Grade 1

The Syllabus of Examinations should be read for details of requirements, especially those for scales, aural tests and sight-reading. Attention should be paid to the Special Notices on the front inside cover, where warning is given of changes.

The syllabus is obtainable from music dealers or from The Associated Board of the Royal Schools of Music, 14 Bedford Square, London WC1B 3JG (please send a stamped addressed C5 envelope).

In overseas centres, information may be obtained from the Local Representative or Resident Secretary.

Requirements

SCALES, ARPEGGIOS AND BROKEN CHORDS
(from memory)

Scales
(i) each hand separately, up and down
     (*or* down and up in L.H. at candidate's choice)
     in the following keys:
     C, G, D, F majors and A, D minors
     (melodic *or* harmonic minor at candidate's choice)
     (all two octaves)
(ii) in contrary motion, both hands beginning and
     ending on the key-note (unison), in the key of
     C major only (one octave)

Arpeggios
the common chords of C, G and F majors,
and A and D minors, in root position only,
each hand separately (one octave)

Broken Chords
formed from the chords of C, G and F majors,
and A and D minors, each hand separately,
according to the pattern shown in the syllabus

PLAYING AT SIGHT (see current syllabus)

AURAL TESTS (see current syllabus)

THREE PIECES

LIST A   *page*
1 **Daniel Gottlob Türk** (1750–1813)
   'Youthful Joy', No. 25 from
   60 Pieces for Aspiring Players, Book I   2
2 **Anton Diabelli** (1781–1858)
   Lesson in C, Op. 125 No. 6   3
3 **Dmitri Kabalevsky** (1904–1987)
   Theme and First Variation, from
   5 Happy Variations on a Russian Folksong,
   Op. 51 No. 1   4

LIST B
1 **George Frideric Handel** (1685–1759)
   Passepied in C, HWV 559   5
2 **Alexander Grechaninov** (1864–1956)
   'Fairy Tale', No. 1 from *Children's Book*, Op. 98   6
3 **Stephen Duro**
   'Rainy Day', No. 6 from *Finger Jogging Boogie*   7

Candidates must prepare Nos. 1 & 2 from the *same* list, A *or* B, but may choose No. 3 from *either* list *or* one of the further alternatives listed below:

Sartorio Two Frogs, Op. 783 No. 12
Matthay Catch Ball, Op. 35 Book 1 No. 3
These are included in A Romantic Sketchbook for Piano, Book I, *published by the Associated Board*

Editor for the Associated Board: **Richard Jones**

Music origination by Barnes Music Engraving Ltd.
Printed in Great Britain by Headley Brothers Ltd,
The Invicta Press, Ashford, Kent and London.

Where appropriate, pieces have been checked with original source material and edited as necessary for instructional purposes. Fingering, phrasing, pedalling, metronome marks and the editorial realization of ornaments (where given) are for guidance but are not comprehensive or obligatory.

A:1

Youthful Joy

No. 25 from *60 Pieces for Aspiring Players*, Book I

TÜRK

Source: *Sechzig Handstücke für angehende Klavierspieler, Erster Theil* (Leipzig and Halle, 1792), No. 25, 'Jugendlich froh'.
Repeats, indicated by repeat marks in the original, are here notated in full. The original staccato dashes and the sign ⸗, which Türk used to indicate the shortening of the last note of a phrase (right hand of bars 4, 12, 20 and 28), have been replaced by staccato dots. All other staccato dots (apart from bars 2, 10, 18 and 26), dynamics and right-hand slurs are editorial suggestions only (left-hand slurs are present in the source).

© 1997 by The Associated Board of the Royal Schools of Music
Selected from Türk, *60 Pieces for Aspiring Players*, Book I, edited by Howard Ferguson (Associated Board)

Lesson in C

Op. 125 No. 6

DIABELLI

Source: *Die ersten 12 Lectionen am Pianoforte*, Op. 125 (London, 1892).
Anton Diabelli (1781–1858) was an Austrian music publisher who wrote the waltz theme for Beethoven's Diabelli Variations. In the Lesson in C slurs and dynamics are adopted from the posthumous source. Since they are presumably editorial suggestions only, they may be treated as optional.

A:3

Theme and First Variation

from *5 Happy Variations on a Russian Folksong*, Op. 51 No. 1

KABALEVSKY

Passepied in C

HWV 559

HANDEL

Source: autograph, Cambridge, Fitzwilliam Museum, 30.H.13., MS 263, p.3 (*c*.1721/2).
This passepied (a kind of slow minuet) belongs to a collection of elementary pieces that Handel used for composition lessons. It also survives in a version in D which he employed in the ballet music and closing chorus of the opera *Radamisto* (London, 1720). Repeats, indicated by repeat signs in the original, are here notated in full. Slurs and dynamics are editorial suggestions only. Unslurred crotchets should be lightly detached.

Fairy Tale

No. 1 from *Children's Book*, Op. 98

GRECHANINOV

Source: *Kinderbuch*, Op. 98 (Mainz and Leipzig, 1924).
Grechaninov (1864–1956), a pupil of Arensky and Rimsky-Korsakov, was a prolific Russian composer who, late in life, moved to Paris and New York. Apart from the *mf* in bar 0, all dynamics are editorial suggestions only.

Rainy Day

No. 6 from *Finger Jogging Boogie*

STEPHEN DURO

B:3